PAGE 4

1 1
2 2
3 3
4 4

PAGE 5

1 1
2 2
3 3
4 4

PAGE 6

1 1 1
2 2 2
3 3
4 4

PAGE 7

1 1 1
4 4 4
3 3
2 2

1 1 1
2 2 2
3 3 3
4 4 4

C C
E E
E I
N N

A A
D E
E E
R R

T T T
I I I
F F
G G

MY FIRST BOOK OF

su doku

NUMBERS, LETTERS, COLORS & SHAPES

by Rafael Sirkis   Illustrated by Daria & Linor Ackerman

Su Doku for Kids! Numbers, Letters & More!
Copyright © 2006 by Rafael Sirkis.

Su Doku for Kids! Shapes, Colors & More!
Copyright © 2006 by Rafael Sirkis.

Patent applications were filed regarding some features of the puzzles included in this book. These patents are pending. All rights reserved. Published by Scholastic Inc. SCHOLASTIC, CARTWHEEL BOOKS, and associated logos are trademarks and/or registered trademarks of Scholastic Inc.

ISBN-13: 978-0-545-00016-1   ISBN-10: 0-545-00016-5

10 9 8 7 6 5 4 3 2 1   07 08 09 10 11

Printed in the U.S.A.
First Scholastic printing, August 2007

Cartwheel BOOKS®

Scholastic Inc.

New York Toronto London Auckland Sydney
Mexico City New Delhi Hong Kong Buenos Aires

Have you ever seen a su doku puzzle before? If not, you are in for a treat! Su doku is a puzzle made popular in Japan. Each puzzle is made up of 4 boxes. Each of these boxes is made of 4 squares. The trick is to fill each box with 4 different picture stickers.

Each picture will be used 4 times in the puzzle, but the same picture CANNOT be used more than ONCE in a row, column, or box.

This is a box.

This is a square.

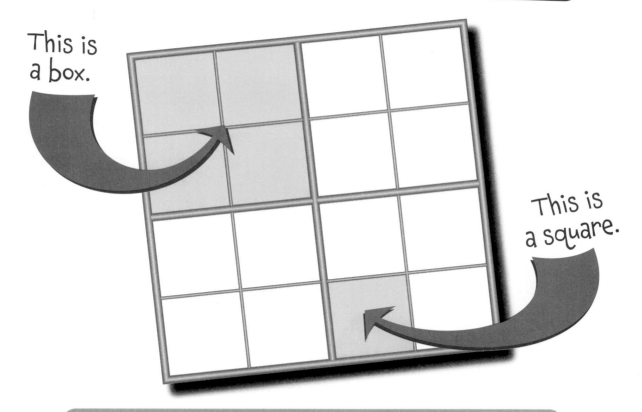

Each su doku puzzle has a different color border that shows its level of difficulty:
GREEN = beginner, YELLOW = medium, and RED = hard.

There are **more than 200 stickers** included in this book!

Use the stickers from each set to complete each puzzle. Each sticker goes in a blank square in the puzzle.

Don't forget: Each picture can appear only ONCE in each row, column, and box!

This is a column.

This is a row.

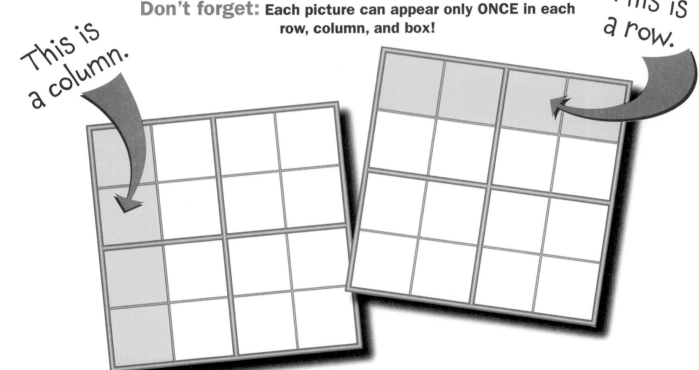

Get ready to solve some su doku puzzles!

Try to solve them all! Use the answer key in the back to help you if you get stuck.

3

	3	4	
2			3
4			1
	1	2	

1 2 3 4

5

1
2
3
4

			1
		3	4
2	4		
3			

6

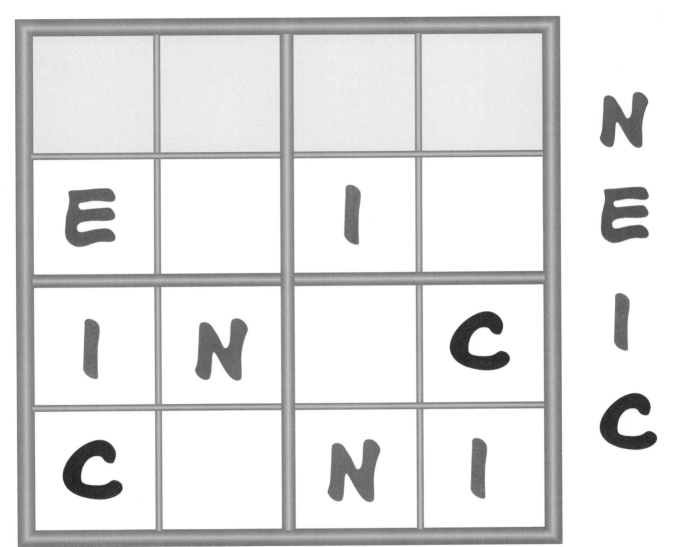

N E I C C

9

The shaded row spells a word!

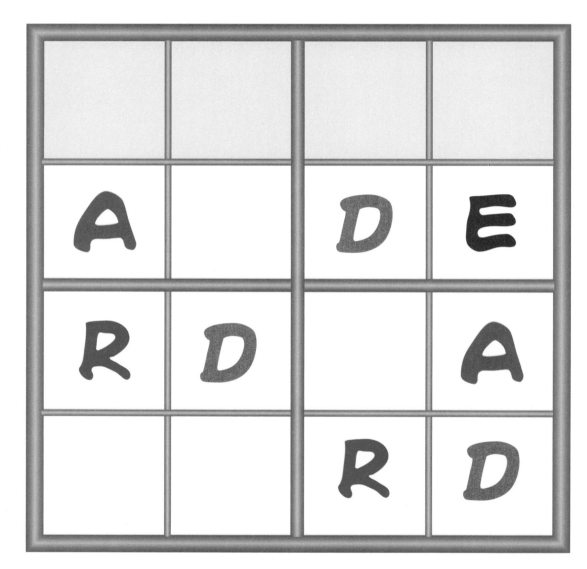

10

The shaded row spells a word!

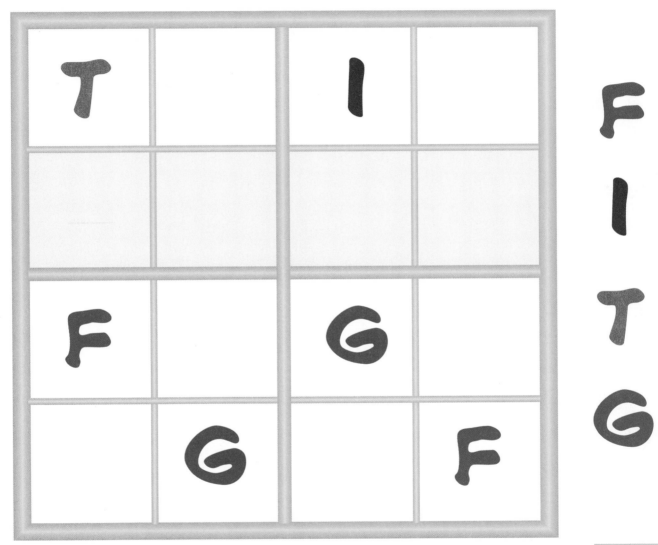

The shaded row spells a word!

11

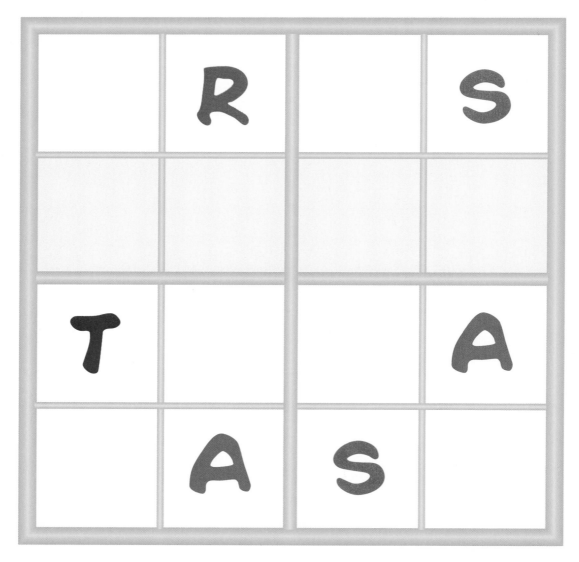

12

The shaded row spells a word!

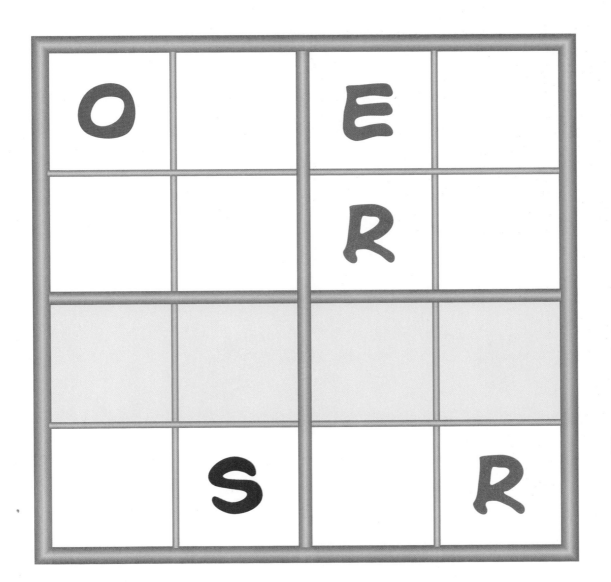

The shaded row spells a word!

13

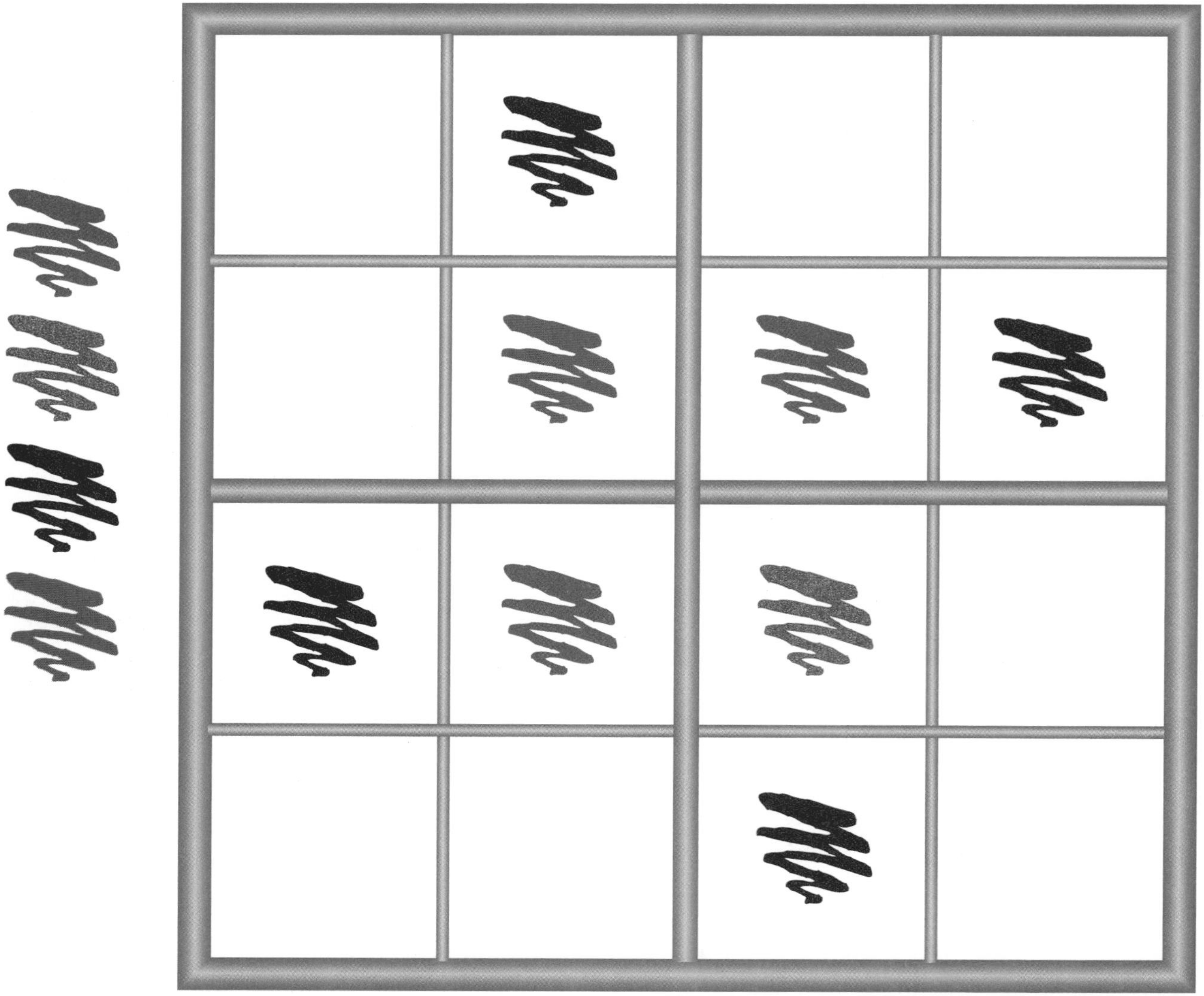

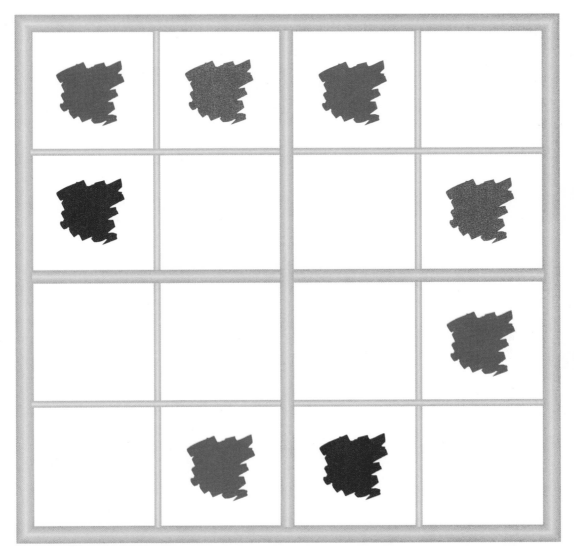

15

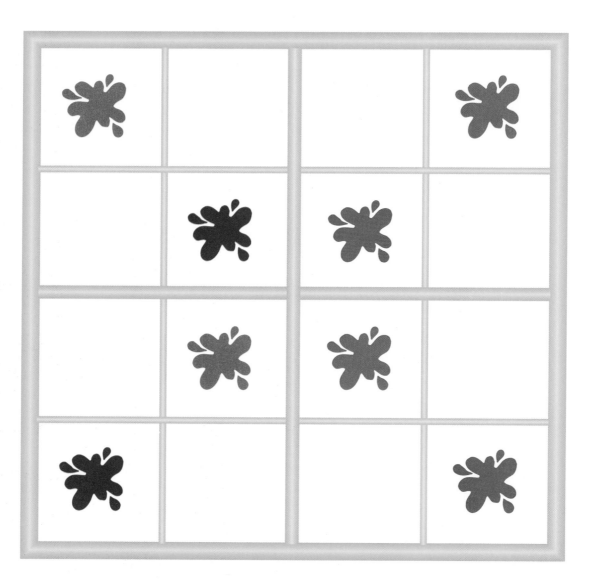

16

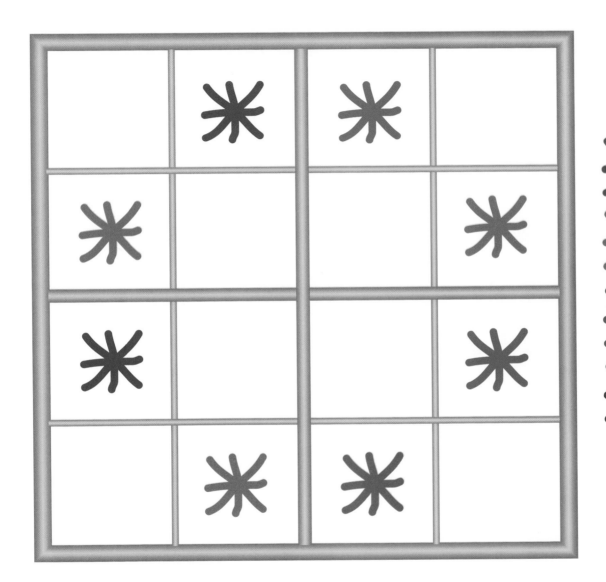

17

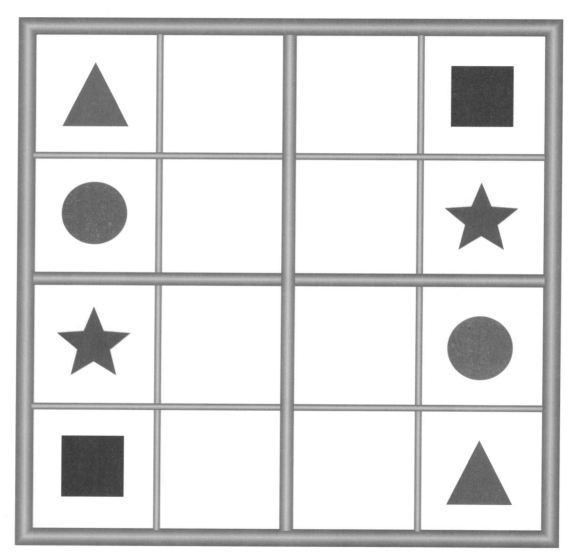

18

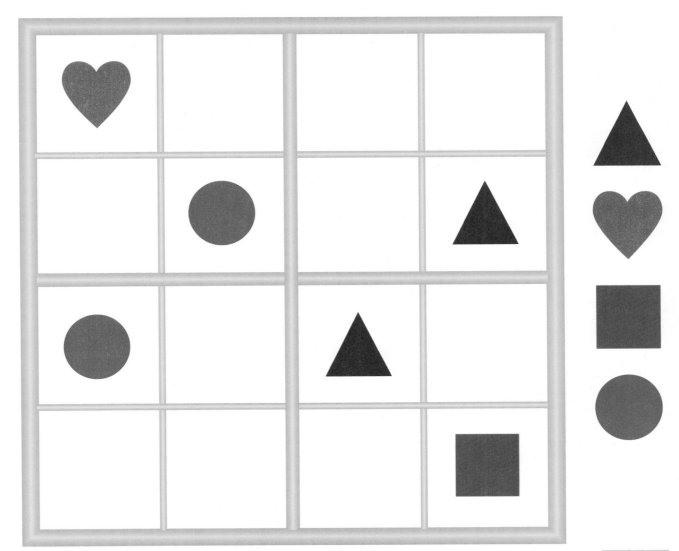

19

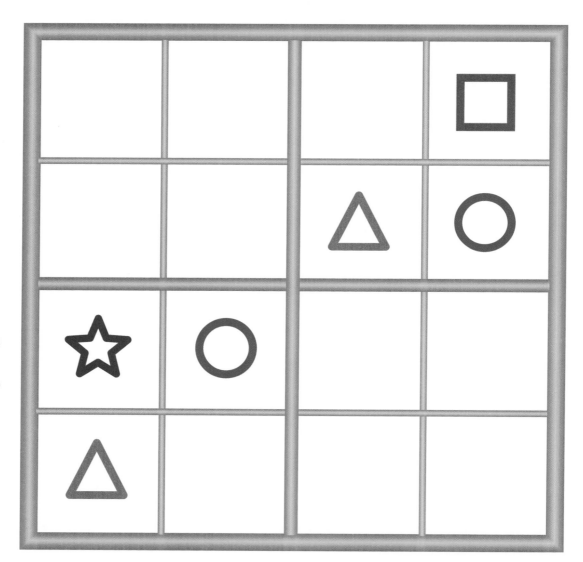

20

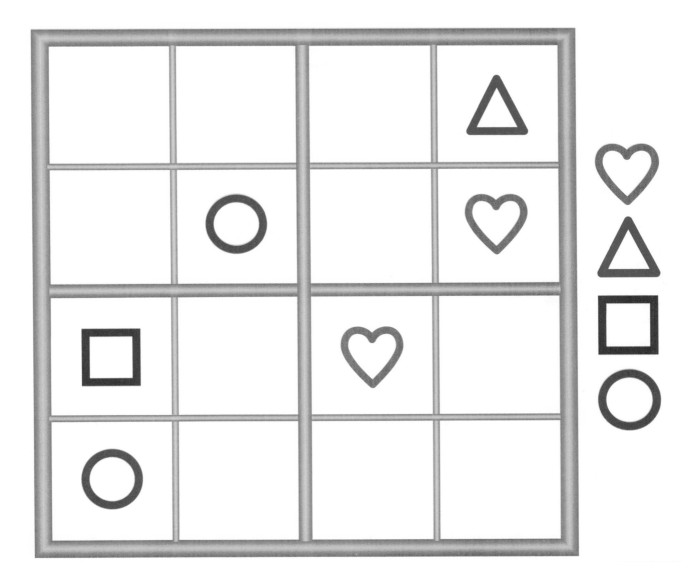

21

Answer Key

pages 4-5

2	3	4	1
1	4	3	2
3	2	1	4
4	1	2	3

1	3	4	2
2	4	1	3
4	2	3	1
3	1	2	4

page 10

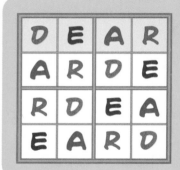

D	E	A	R
A	R	D	E
R	D	E	A
E	A	R	D

pages 6-7

4	3	2	1
1	2	3	4
2	4	1	3
3	1	4	2

2	4	3	1
1	3	4	2
4	1	2	3
3	2	1	4

page 12

A	R	T	S
S	T	A	R
T	S	R	A
R	A	S	T

pages 8-9

2	1	3	4
4	3	1	2
3	4	2	1
1	2	4	3

N	I	C	E
E	C	I	N
I	N	E	C
C	E	N	I

page 14

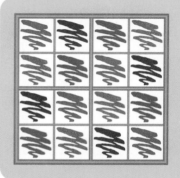

22

Answer Key

page 11

T	F	I	G
G	I	F	T
F	T	G	I
I	G	T	F

pages 16–17

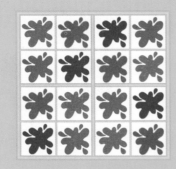

page 13

O	R	E	S
S	E	R	O
R	O	S	E
E	S	O	R

pages 18–19

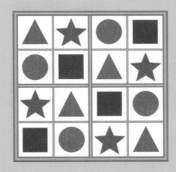

page 15

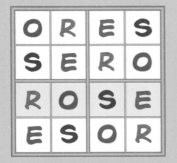

pages 20–21

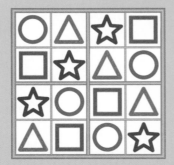

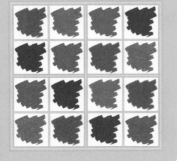

23

Congratulations

on solving your very first su doku puzzles!

PAGE 12

R R R

T T T

A A

S S

PAGE 13

E E E

O O O

S S S

R R

PAGE 14

PAGE 15

PAGE 16

ISBN: S-T25-00016-5

PAGE 17

PAGE 18

PAGE 19

PAGE 20

PAGE 21